The Big Cats

Willie Ortiz

Published by Willie Ortiz
Using CreateSpace.com
Printed in USA

ISBN:1979741123
ISBN-13:9781979741125

Tigers

The Tiger is the largest of all the big cats. Tigers can stand between 4.5 feet – 9.5 feet tall with a tail length of 2 – 4 feet and can weigh between 400 – 675 lbs. The Sumatran tiger is the smallest of the tigers weighing around 220 – 310 lbs. Tigers can run up to 40 mph in short bursts. Tigers eat samber deer, wild pigs, water buffalo, antelope, sloth bears, leopards, dogs, crocodiles, pythons, monkeys and hares. Tigers in the wild can live from 10-15 years. A tiger can leap more than 30 feet. A tiger's stripes are like a tattoo; they go all the way down to their skin.

Tigers are excellent swimmers and they constantly need water to stay hydrated. Tigers also like water because they have such thick fur and they need to cool off.

Sumatran tigers have the most stripes of all tigers. Siberian tigers have the least number of stripes. Sumatran tiger's stripes are narrower than other species of tigers and they also have larger manes. Adult tigers have 30 teeth. Sumatran tigers have slightly webbed paws which allow them to swim more efficiently after prey. The word tiger came from the Greek work "tigris", which is derived from a Persian word that means arrow, comparing the speed of the animal and an arrow, or because of the Tigris River. Sumatran tigers are the smallest subspecies of tiger in the world.

There are nine subspecies of tigers in the world, four of which are extinct.

Bengal - Less than 2,000 left in the wild   Siberian -450 left in the wild
Indochinese- 750-1,300 left in the wild   South Chinese -Extinct in the wild
Sumatran- 400-50 left in the wild   Malayan -600-800 left in the wild
Caspian- Extinct   Javan -Extinct
Bali -Extinct

Florida alone is home to a reported 1,455 privately owned tigers at a time when there are only around 5000 tigers left in the wild.

Poaching is the most serious threat to tigers. Every part of the tiger is traded in illegal wildlife black markets. Parts of just one tiger can fetch up to $50,000 on these black markets. Body parts are used in traditional Asian medicine. Their pelts are viewed as status symbols, creating an increased demand, which increases poaching. According to the wildlife trade network.TRAFFIC about 1,000 tigers have been killed in the past 10 years for illegal trade to meet consumer demand in Asia.

Lions

The word lion comes from the Latin word Leo and the ancient Greek work leon. Lions are the second largest cat only to tigers and they live 10-15 years in the wild. Lions are apex predators although over 50% of their food comes from scavenging. They eat wildebeest, impala, zebra, giraffe, buffalo, wild hogs, and sometimes they will eat rhinoceros, hippopotamus, and elephants if hungry enough. Lions hunt mostly at night and sleep most of the day. Habitat loss and conflicts with humans are the biggest reasons for the decline in the lion's numbers. White lions owe their coloring to a recessive allele; they are rare forms of the subspecies Panthera leo krugeri.

Lions are one of five in the genus Panthera and a member of the family Felidae. There are 8 subspecies of lions and they are:

Addis Ababa aka Ethiopian lion	West African lion aka Senegal lion
Masai lion aka East African lion	Congo lion aka Northeast Congo lion
Southwest African lion aka Katanga lion	Transvaal lion aka Southeast African lion

Barbary lion aka Atlas lion or North African Lion Extinct.
Asiatic lion aka Indian lion or Persian lion less than 523 remain in the wild.

A pride of lionesses takes up identical spots in the hunting formation each time like the positions of players on a football team.

The mighty lion once roamed throughout all of Africa. Overtime 80 percent of their historical habitat has been lost to the increase human population. They now live in only 28 African countries and India. Farmers frequently kill lions because they believe them as a threat to the livestock. Farmland also destroys the lions' habitat, confining them to small pockets of land. People also overhunt the lions' prey, which causes a shortage available food sources for the lion.

Unlike other cats, lions are very social animals. They live in groups, called prides, of around 30 lions. A pride consists of up to three males, a dozen related females, and their young. The size of the pride is determined by the availability of food and water.

Leopard

The leopard is a member of the Felidae family. Leopards are found in regions of sub-Saharan Africa, West Asia, the Middle East, South and Southeast Asia to Siberia. The black coloration (melanism) is found in some mammal species, especially big cats, where individuals that normally have patterns or stripes in their coat are instead completely black. This happens in most species of cats except for Tigers and Lions. Melanism is the name of the dark color pigmentation mutation in a jaguar or leopard that cause the fur to be blackish, it occurs in about 6% of the population of big cats.

The animal known as a "panther" actually refers to 3 different types of big cats, leopards, jaguars, and cougars. Each has a black or white color mutation. The melanism gene is a dominant gene in jaguars, a black jaguar may produce either black or spotted cubs, while a pair of spotted jaguars can only have spotted cubs. Black leopards are more common in Asia than in Africa.

The black panther is often called 'the ghost of the forest'. It is a very smart, stealth-like predator, with its dark coat the black panther can hide and stalk prey very easily at night. Black panthers are great swimmers. They are one of the strongest tree climbing big cats, often pouncing on prey from a tree. Panthers are capable of leaping up to 20 feet to catch their prey, which includes medium sized animals like deer and monkeys and smaller rabbits and birds. Black panthers have good hearing, extremely good eyesight, and a strong jaw.

Cheetahs

Wild cheetahs are found in eastern and southwestern Africa. There are about 7,000 of these big cats remain in the wild and are under pressure as the wide-open grasslands are disappearing at the hands of human settlers. Cheetahs are the only big cat that can turn in midair while sprinting. The cheetah originated over four million years ago, making them the oldest of the big cats. Cheetahs pray on antelopes, gazelles, warthogs, porcupines, and various bird including ostriches. At the height of an intense chase cheetahs body temperatures can reach 105 degrees Fahrenheit.

Cheetah's once ranged from India, through the Middle East and extended to the very south of the African continent. Today, to the north, the Asian cheetah is almost extinct and can only be found in a few remote areas of Iran and Afghanistan. It is believed that due to its reduced numbers the cheetah is also threatened genetically from inbreeding, reducing the animal's immunity from disease.

A cheetah can cover 23-26 feet in just one stride.

Jaguars

The jaguar is a feline in the Panthera genus and is the only surviving panther species native to the Americas. The jaguar is the third largest feline behind the tiger and lion. The jaguar most closely resembles the leopard physically although the jaguar is larger and sturdier. The jaguar's behavior and habitat characteristics resemble the tiger's as it prefers dense rainforest.

The jaguar will range across a variety of forested and open terrains. Just like the tiger, juguars loves water. The Jaguar is a solitary, opportunistic, ambush predator at the top of the food chain. It is a keystone species playing an important part in stabilizing ecosystems and regulating the populations of its prey. The Jaguar is a near threatened species due to habitat loss and although international trade of parts is prohibited the cat is still killed by humans especially in conflicts with ranchers and farmers in South America.

Jaguar, the car company, began in 1922 in a factory operated by a British outfit named Swallow Sidecar and Coach Building Company, initially a manufacturer of motorcycle sidecars. Swallow owner William Lyons Bought out his partner in 1934 and switched the company name to SS Cars Limited and produced two seat sports cars. In 1935, Lyons chose the name Jaguar for his newest model car because of its association with the strength, elegance, and smooth agility of the jungle cat. In 1937 the automobile added its now famous leaping Jaguar hood ornament. In 1945, the company officially changed their name to Jaguar Cars Unlimited.

The Jaguar has featured prominently in the mythology of numerous indigenous American cultures, including those of the Maya and Aztec. According to legend the jaguar has the ability to travel between spiritual realms. Jaguar gums and jaws adjacent to the four primary killing teeth are threaded with pressure sensitive nerves that help locate the right spot to execute prey.   Thierr tongues are lined with sharp protuberances which help remove flesh from cartilage and bones. Jaguars have the biggest brain to body mass of all the big cats.

Jaguars digestive tract, like those of other felines are designed to process meat exclusively. Jaguars do not sweat and can overheat easily.

Snow Leopards

Snow leopards can live from 15-20 years in the wild and are native to the mountain ranges of Central and South Asia. They can weigh about 60-165 lbs. and their length from head to tail is about 30-60 inches. When hunting Snow Leopards like to strike from above using rocks and brushes as concealment until the prey is nearby. Once their prey is in range the snow leopard will pounce with an unsuspecting attack.

Snow leopard are built for surviving in the cold, rocky, mountain ranges. The snow leopard's tail is long and flexible to help with their balance. Their tails are very thick made of fat storage with heavy thick fur. This furry long tail can wrapped around their face and body to stay warm while sleeping. Snow leopards have stocky bodies with thick fur. Even their ears are short and rounded all of which help to minimize heat loss. The snow leopard's paws are wide for better walking in the snow. They also have fur on the bottoms to increase their grip on steep and slippery surfaces. This fur under the paws also minimizes heat loss too.

Snow leopards are opportunistic feeders eating whatever meat they can find including carrion (dead or decayed flesh of an animal), domestic livestock, bharal (blue sheep), Himalayan Tahr (large goat like animal), horse, camel, hares, and birds. Snow leopards also eat a lot of vegetation including grass and twigs.

Clouded Leopards

Clouded leopards are two species of wild cat that live throughout the forests of Southeast Asia. The smallest of the big cats, they are secretive and rare in the wild, preferring to remain alone and hidden from view. Clouded leopards live in lowland tropical rainforests, dry woodlands, and secondary forests. They have been spotted at elevations up to 9000 feet in the Himalayan Mountains. Historically, their range covered most of Southeast Asia from Nepal and southern China, Thailand, Indonesia, and Borneo. However, this range has shrunk due to habitat destruction and human poaching.

In China, the clouded leopard is known as the 'Mint Leopard' because its spots can also look like mint leaves. These cats usually stand 10-16 inches tall and are 4 to 6 feet long with tails almost the length of their bodies. Males tend to be larger and weigh up to 50 pounds, while females weigh about 35 pounds. Clouded leopards live to about 10-15 years old in wild.

In their appearance, the Sunda clouded leopard have smaller and darker cloud markings and a darker overall coat color. Most clouded leopard pictures are from mainland nebulosa individuals, meaning that the Sunda clouded leopard are much rarer. Wild Sunda clouded leopards were only first caught on video in early 2010.

Cougars

Cougars are native to Asia, America, and Africa. The common habitat is the coniferous and tropical forests, swamps, or grasslands. The diet of Cougars consists of large mammals, including deer, but they also eat smaller animals including rabbits and birds. Cougars also have similar body types to house cats, only on a much larger scale. They have slender bodies and round heads with pointed ears. They are about 5-9 ft. from head to tail. While males can weigh up to 150 lb., females weigh less, topping out at nearly 100 lbs. A healthy cougar in the wild can live to around 10 years of age.

An American feline resembles the African panther in size and habits. The cougar's color is tawny, without spots and occasionally referred to as the American lion and known as Puma, Mountain Lion, Catamount, or Panther. The Florida panther has adapted to the subtropical forests and swamp environments. However they are very rare animals, as of 2013 it is believed only 160 Florida panthers remain in the wild mostly is southern part of the state.

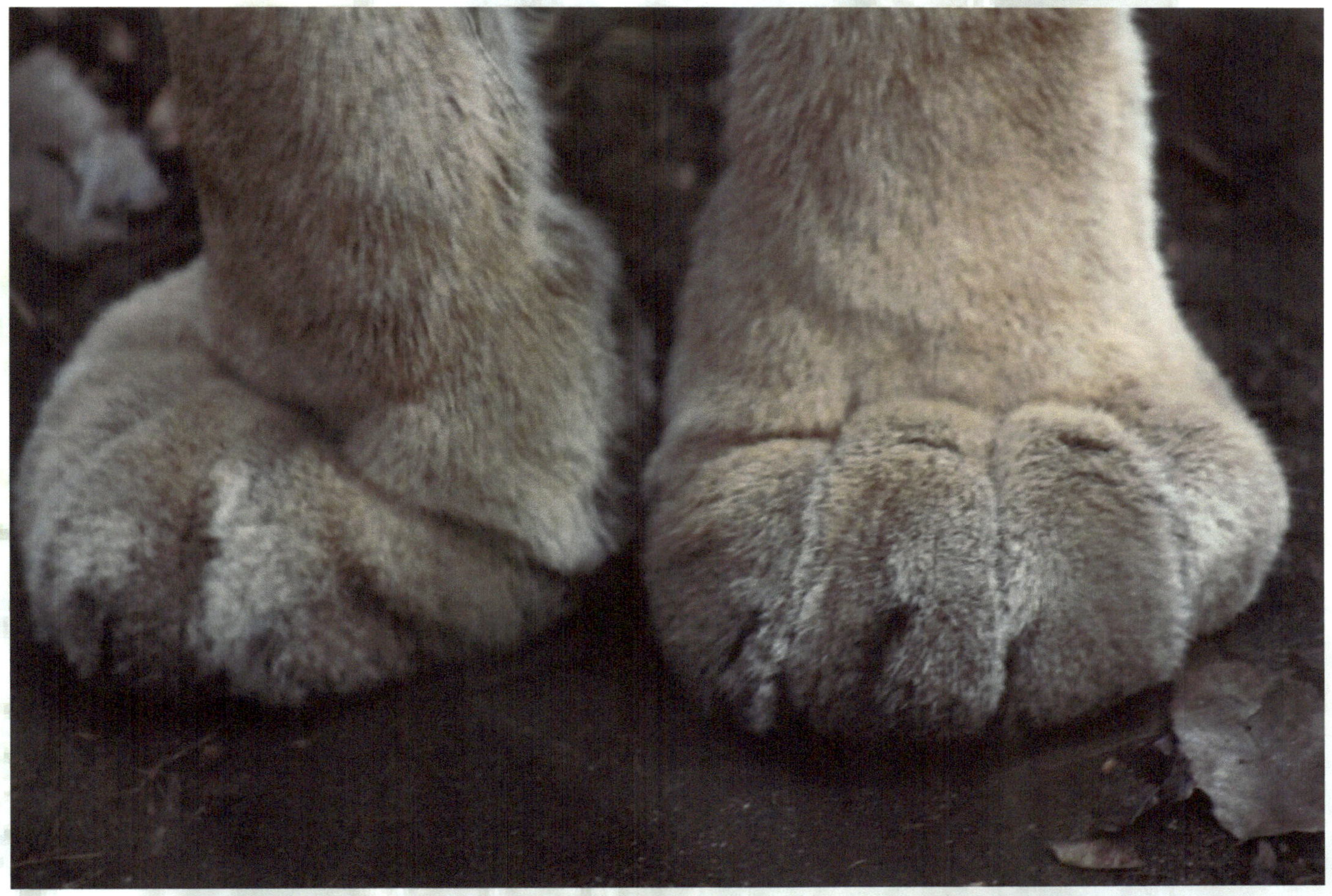

Cougars have no natural enemies and they sit on top of the food chain. However, they occasionally compete with other predators such as bears and wolves for food. During most of their lives, cougars are solitary creatures. They interact only to mate, which can happen at any time of year. Females can breed as early as 2-3 years old and give birth to 2-3 kittens at a time. They raise their young while the males return to their solitary lifestyles. When the cubs reach two years old, they will leave their mother to start their own life. Some travel far to establish their own territory as cougars need a lot of room to roam.

The End

```
Q V T Q X A Z K U M E B M I E M J O
F U N M C B L U Y H H G H Z C G C Y
W V I S K T K R O U D T H K Y C L W
S O Q N M S E D H L W G V B L M O E
Q T F R W V N W Q A D U W R Q T U E
I E A L E E I O P Y S C G A H L D R
X R S C P G U J W M B Y E G Q E E O
K N E M G N I E Q L R T T U F J D K
I Q R H F I N T U A E X T O D P L A
N Q C G T R B G U M O O S C X B E J
M R A J F N E G F Q F C P R K F O E
A V P V C T A K Z C R S V A S V P T
H V A L A J S P A P W Y R C R R A U
X I Q X L E O P A R D I G R Q D R C
E Q C I S A U U N R U R B Q G P D V
I T L B P M N A N K I X N O I L M L
U W C L T U O G I M B D N I Y Z B E
T H B V C P U S R R J N G K J G M S
```

BIG CATS
LEOPARD
SNOW LEOPARD
CLOUDED LEOPARD
LION
TIGER
COUGAR
PANTHER
JAGUAR
PUMA

About the Author

Willie Ortiz is an avid wildlife, nature, and travel photographer. He has traveled extensively across Asia, Europe, and the Americas to view and photograph animals in their natural habitat. When the natural habitat is almost impossible, Willie is a patron of animal rehabilitation and education centers. Animals of Belize, Willie's first book truly shows the passion he has for protecting wildlife through education. Willie's photography reflects his love of nature and expresses a unique perspective of history, nature, and the world around us. Willie's catalog of books includes children's educational, travel, nature, and history themes. Willie Ortiz is originally from the Bronx and currently resides on the Treasure Coast of Florida.